Ice Cream

UNDER THE INFLUENCE

Becky Rasmussen

BLUEPRINT PRESS
INTERNATIONALE

ISBN
978-1-961117-24-2 (Paperback)
978-1-961117-25-9 (eBook)
978-1-961117-23-5 (Hardcover)

For my Scrapbooking Girls - my always supportive and eager taste testers.

CONTENTS

**Section 4 Drinks For Everyone
(Alcohol-Free Versions)................ 55**

INTRODUCTION

We All Scream For Ice Cream...Drinks!

Plain and simple, ice cream drinks are impressive. When you go to a restaurant and order an ice cream drink, whether it's a malt, shake or drink from the bar, they always look amazing when the server appears with your order. And they taste as good as they look.

Ice cream drinks are not difficult to prepare at home. You don't need fancy equipment or bartending experience to create delicious frozen drinks. Simple equipment like a hand mixer, spatula and an extra large mixing bowl are all you need to make these delicious treats.

The recipes in this book can be prepared ahead of time to make serving your favorite ice cream beverage a breeze. Here are some tips to keep in mind when preparing and serving ice cream drinks.

Make Ahead Then Thaw

Making drinks ahead of time can save you a lot of time. However, you will need to allow time for drinks to thaw to the desired consistency.

All the recipes in this book can be made ahead of time and kept frozen in a freezer safe storage container until you are ready to serve them. Thawing time will depend on the size of the batch and depth of the container. Allow for a minimum of 30 minutes thawing time for a small batch and at least 45 minutes for a large batch. Uncovering and stirring the mixture will speed up the melting process.

The Wow Factor

The Wow Factor of an ice cream drink is in the garnish. Just like a good Bloody Mary, a garnish adds a little personality to your ice cream drink creation. Suggested garnishes include: Whipped Cream, Cookies, Fruit, Sprinkles, Candies, Flavored Syrups and Breakfast Cereal. However, you get extra credit for using your imagination, so feel free to get creative while garnishing. Just make sure whatever you use to garnish your drinks is edible.

Liqueurs, Vodkas & Rums. Oh My!

There is a plethora of flavored alcohol varieties available. The recipes in this book call for many different combinations. Vodka, Schnapps, Liqueur and Rum types are interchangeable. However, substitutions will change the flavor of the ice cream drink. Below are substitution notes you should be aware of before making a change.

<u>**Rums:**</u> When substituting with a flavored rum you are getting both the fruit flavor and the rum flavor. Rum substitutions will work best in fruity themed drinks.

<u>**Vodkas:**</u> Vodka typically has a much stronger alcohol aftertaste than liqueurs and schnapps. **Be careful**: adding too much vodka to the ice cream mixture will give it a heavy aftertaste.

<u>**Liqueurs and Schnapps:**</u> Liqueurs and Schnapps work very well in ice cream mixtures and are good substitutes for vodkas and rums.

<u>**Whiskeys, Bourbons and Scotches:**</u> Whiskeys, Bourbons and Scotches have very potent flavors and strong aftertastes, so they are not an interchangeable substitute. However, they can complement the flavors of an ice cream drink. Add slowly

so they do not overpower the flavors in your ice cream drink. I recommend starting with ¼ cup (large batch) or ¼ oz (small batch) increments. You can always add more.

Kick It Up A Notch

If you would like your ice cream drinks to pack a little more punch, the recipes in the book can easily be altered. Adding up to an additional cup of liquor to a large batch of ice cream will give your drinks a little more kick. Or try making your own creations by adding your favorite flavors. Stick to a 3 cup alcohol maximum to allow ice cream mixture to set (3 oz. small batch maximum). Most importantly, please remember to be responsible!

Alcohol-Free Versions

Even if you do not drink alcohol, there are still lots of good reasons to enjoy a delicious ice cream drink. Section 4 of this cookbook contains alcohol-free versions of some of the provided recipes. They do taste a little different than the original versions, but are enjoyable just as well and family friendly.

Large Batch & Small Batch Recipes

In case a whole gallon of ice cream drinks is too much for the occasion or too big for your freezer, the recipes in this book contain both large batch and small batch ingredient amounts.

OTHER WAYS TO DRESS UP YOUR DRINK

Just in case edible garnishes aren't enough, here are a few more ideas to take your drinks to the next level.

- Swizzle Sticks
- Fun Straws
- Umbrellas
- Candles
- Decorated Toothpicks
- Edible Glitter
- Spoons! – Remember thawing is optional!

For Chocolate Lovers

Chocolate Mint Hoppers

CHOCOLATE MINT HOPPERS

Ingredients

Large Batch	Small Batch
1 Gallon Chocolate Ice Cream	2 Cups Chocolate Ice Cream
16 oz. Cool Whip™	1/2 Cup Cool Whip™
1 Cup Crème de Menthe	1 oz. Crème de Menthe
1 Cup Chocolate Liqueur	1 oz. Chocolate Liqueur

Instructions

- Remove ice cream and Cool Whip™ from freezer ahead of time. Cool Whip™ should be completely thawed before using. Ice cream should be soft enough to mix with an electric hand mixer. In an extra large mixing bowl, blend ice cream until smooth. Combine crème de menthe and chocolate liqueur with ice cream and mix until fully blended. Using a spatula, gently fold in Cool Whip™. Place mixture in a freezer safe container and freeze for at least 24 hours prior to serving.

- Remove from freezer and uncover at least 45 minutes (30 minutes small batch) prior to serving if you want to enjoy using a straw. If using spoons, ice cream can be enjoyed immediately.

Garnish Ideas: Whipped Cream, Chocolate Mint Candies, Chocolate Shavings & Mint Cookies

CHOCOLATE SALTED CARAMEL TWISTS

Ingredients

Large Batch	Small Batch
1 Gallon Chocolate Ice Cream	2 Cups Chocolate Ice Cream
16 oz. Cool Whip™	1/2 Cup Cool Whip™
1 ½ Cups Salted Carmel Cream Liqueur	1 ½ oz. Salted Carmel Cream Liqueur
1 Cup Chocolate Liqueur	1 oz. Chocolate Liqueur

Instructions

- Remove ice cream and Cool Whip™ from freezer ahead of time. Cool Whip™ should be completely thawed before using. Ice cream should be soft enough to mix with an electric hand mixer. In an extra large mixing bowl, blend ice cream until smooth. Combine salted caramel cream liqueur and chocolate liqueur with ice cream and mix until fully blended. Using a spatula, gently fold in Cool Whip™. Place mixture in a freezer safe container and freeze for at least 24 hours prior to serving.

- Remove from freezer and uncover at least 45 minutes (30 minutes small batch) prior to serving if you want to enjoy using a straw. If using spoons, ice cream can be enjoyed immediately.

Garnish Ideas: Whipped Cream, Carmel Syrup, Pretzels & Coconut Caramel Cookies

TRIPLE CHOCOLATE OVERLOAD

Ingredients

Large Batch	Small Batch
1 Gallon Chocolate Ice Cream	2 Cups Chocolate Ice Cream
16 oz. Cool Whip™	½ Cup Cool Whip™
1 Cup Crème de Cacao	1 oz. Crème de Cacao
1 Cup Chocolate Liqueur	1 oz. Chocolate Liqueur

Instructions

- Remove ice cream and Cool Whip™ from freezer ahead of time. Cool Whip™ should be completely thawed before using. Ice cream should be soft enough to mix with an electric hand mixer. In an extra large mixing bowl, blend ice cream until smooth. Combine crème de cacao and chocolate liqueur with ice cream and mix until fully blended. Using a spatula, gently fold in Cool Whip™. Place mixture in a freezer safe container and freeze for at least 24 hours prior to serving.

- Remove from freezer and uncover at least 45 minutes (30 minutes small batch) prior to serving if you want to enjoy using a straw. If using spoons, ice cream can be enjoyed immediately.

Garnish Ideas: Whipped Cream, Chocolate Syrup, Chocolate Shavings & Chocolate Fudge Cookies

CHOCOLATE PEANUT BUTTER CREAM

Ingredients

Large Batch	Small Batch
1 Gallon Chocolate Ice Cream	2 Cups Chocolate Ice Cream
16 oz. Cool Whip™	½ Cup Cool Whip™
1 ½ Cups Peanut Butter Cream Liqueur	1 ½ oz. Peanut Butter Cream Liqueur
1 Cup Chocolate Liqueur	1 oz. Chocolate Liqueur

Instructions

- Remove ice cream and Cool Whip™ from freezer ahead of time. Cool Whip™ should be completely thawed before using. Ice cream should be soft enough to mix with an electric hand mixer. In an extra large mixing bowl, blend ice cream until smooth. Combine peanut butter cream liqueur and chocolate liqueur with ice cream and mix until fully blended. Using a spatula, gently fold in Cool Whip™. Place mixture in a freezer safe container and freeze for at least 24 hours prior to serving.

- Remove from freezer and uncover at least 45 minutes (30 minutes small batch) prior to serving if you want to enjoy using a straw. If using spoons, ice cream can be enjoyed immediately.

Garnish Ideas: Whipped Cream, Chocolate Syrup, Chocolate Shavings & Peanut Butter Cup Candies

LET'S GO BANANAS

Ingredients

Large Batch	Small Batch
1 Gallon Chocolate Ice Cream	2 Cups Chocolate Ice Cream
16 oz. Cool Whip™	½ Cup Cool Whip™
1 Cup Banana Liqueur	1 oz. Banana Liqueur
1 Cup Chocolate Liqueur	1 oz. Chocolate Liqueur

Instructions

- Remove ice cream and Cool Whip™ from freezer ahead of time. Cool Whip™ should be completely thawed before using. Ice cream should be soft enough to mix with an electric hand mixer. In an extra large mixing bowl, blend ice cream until smooth. Combine banana liqueur and chocolate liqueur with ice cream and mix until fully blended. Using a spatula, gently fold in Cool Whip™. Place mixture in a freezer safe container and freeze for at least 24 hours prior to serving.

- Remove from freezer and uncover at least 45 minutes (30 minutes small batch) prior to serving if you want to enjoy using a straw. If using spoons, ice cream can be enjoyed immediately.

> **Garnish Ideas:** Whipped Cream, Chocolate Syrup, Chocolate Shavings, Chocolate Cookies & Banana Slices

Ice Cream Under The Influence

DARK CHOCOLATE CARAMEL

Ingredients

Large Batch	Small Batch
1 Gallon Chocolate Ice Cream	2 Cups Chocolate Ice Cream
16 oz. Cool Whip™	½ Cup Cool Whip™
1 Cup Carmel Liqueur	1 oz. Carmel Liqueur
1 Cup Dark Chocolate Liqueur	1 oz. Dark Chocolate Liqueur

Instructions

- Remove ice cream and Cool Whip™ from freezer ahead of time. Cool Whip™ should be completely thawed before using. Ice cream should be soft enough to mix with an electric hand mixer. In an extra large mixing bowl, blend ice cream until smooth. Combine caramel liqueur and dark chocolate liqueur with ice cream and mix until fully blended. Using a spatula, gently fold in Cool Whip™. Place mixture in a freezer safe container and freeze for at least 24 hours prior to serving.

- Remove from freezer and uncover at least 45 minutes (30 minutes small batch) prior to serving if you want to enjoy using a straw. If using spoons, ice cream can be enjoyed immediately.

> **Garnish Ideas:** Whipped Cream, Chocolate Syrup, Caramel Syrup, Chocolate Shavings, Chocolate & Carmel Cookies

CHOCOLATE HAZELNUT

Ingredients

Large Batch	Small Batch
1 Gallon Chocolate Ice Cream	2 Cups Chocolate Ice Cream
16 oz. Cool Whip™	½ Cup Cool Whip™
1 ½ Cups Hazelnut Rum	1 ½ oz. Cups Hazelnut Rum
1 Cup Chocolate Liqueur	1 oz. Chocolate Liqueur

Instructions

- Remove ice cream and Cool Whip™ from freezer ahead of time. Cool Whip™ should be completely thawed before using. Ice cream should be soft enough to mix with an electric hand mixer. In an extra large mixing bowl, blend ice cream until smooth. Combine hazelnut rum and chocolate liqueur with ice cream and mix until fully blended. Using a spatula, gently fold in Cool Whip™. Place mixture in a freezer safe container and freeze for at least 24 hours prior to serving.

- Remove from freezer and uncover at least 45 minutes (30 minutes small batch) prior to serving if you want to enjoy using a straw. If using spoons, ice cream can be enjoyed immediately.

Garnish Ideas: Whipped Cream, Chocolate Syrup & Chocolate Shavings

CHOCOLATE ALMOND HAPPINESS

Ingredients

Large Batch	Small Batch
1 Gallon Chocolate Ice Cream	2 Cups Chocolate Ice Cream
16 oz. Cool Whip™	½ Cup Cool Whip™
1 Cup Almond Cream Liqueur	1 oz. Almond Cream Liqueur
1 Cup Chocolate Liqueur	1 oz. Chocolate Liqueur
2 oz. Almond Extract	1 ½ Tsp. Almond Extract

Instructions

- Remove ice cream and Cool Whip™ from freezer ahead of time. Cool Whip™ should be completely thawed before using. Ice cream should be soft enough to mix with an electric hand mixer. In an extra large mixing bowl, blend ice cream until smooth. Combine almond cream liqueur, chocolate liqueur and almond extract with ice cream and mix until fully blended. Using a spatula, gently fold in Cool Whip™. Place mixture in a freezer safe container and freeze for at least 24 hours prior to serving.

- Remove from freezer and uncover at least 45 minutes (30 minutes small batch) prior to serving if you want to enjoy using a straw. If using spoons, ice cream can be enjoyed immediately.

> **Garnish Ideas:** Whipped Cream, Chocolate Syrup, Chocolate Shavings & Chocolate Fudge Cookies

CHOCOLATE CHIP SUNDAES

Ingredients

Large Batch	Small Batch
1 Gallon Chocolate Chip Ice Cream	2 Cups Chocolate Chip Ice Cream
16 oz. Cool Whip™	½ Cup Cool Whip™
1 Cup Whipped Cream Vodka	1 oz. Whipped Cream Vodka
1 Cup White Chocolate Liqueur	1 oz. White Chocolate Liqueur

Instructions

- Remove ice cream and Cool Whip™ from freezer ahead of time. Cool Whip™ should be completely thawed before using. Ice cream should be soft enough to mix with an electric hand mixer. In an extra large mixing bowl, blend ice cream until smooth. Combine whipped cream vodka and white chocolate liqueur with ice cream and mix until fully blended. Using a spatula, gently fold in Cool Whip™. Place mixture in a freezer safe container and freeze for at least 24 hours prior to serving.

- Remove from freezer and uncover at least 45 minutes (30 minutes small batch) prior to serving if you want to enjoy using a straw. If using spoons, ice cream can be enjoyed immediately.

> **Garnish Ideas:** Whipped Cream, Chocolate Syrup, Maraschino Cherries & Mini Chocolate Chips

FRIGID TURTLES

Ingredients

Large Batch	Small Batch
1 Gallon Butter Pecan Ice Cream	2 Cups Butter Pecan Ice Cream
16 oz. Cool Whip™	½ Cup Cool Whip™
1 Cup Carmel Liqueur	1 oz. Carmel Liqueur
1 Cup Chocolate Liqueur	1 oz. Chocolate Liqueur

Instructions

- Remove ice cream and Cool Whip™ from freezer ahead of time. Cool Whip™ should be completely thawed before using. Ice cream should be soft enough to mix with an electric hand mixer. In an extra large mixing bowl, blend ice cream until smooth. Combine caramel liqueur and chocolate liqueur with ice cream and mix until fully blended. Using a spatula, gently fold in Cool Whip™. Place mixture in a freezer safe container and freeze for at least 24 hours prior to serving.

- Remove from freezer and uncover at least 45 minutes (30 minutes small batch) prior to serving if you want to enjoy using a straw. If using spoons, ice cream can be enjoyed immediately.

Garnish Ideas: Whipped Cream, Chocolate Syrup, Carmel Syrup, Maraschino Cherries & Pecans

DARK CHOCOLATE COCONUT

Ingredients

Large Batch	Small Batch
1 Gallon Chocolate Ice Cream	2 Cups Chocolate Ice Cream
16 oz. Cool Whip™	½ Cup Cool Whip™
1 Cup Coconut Rum	1 oz. Coconut Rum
1 Cup Dark Chocolate Liqueur	1 oz. Dark Chocolate Liqueur

Instructions

- Remove ice cream and Cool Whip™ from freezer ahead of time. Cool Whip™ should be completely thawed before using. Ice cream should be soft enough to mix with an electric hand mixer. In an extra large mixing bowl, blend ice cream until smooth. Combine coconut rum and dark chocolate liqueur with ice cream and mix until fully blended. Using a spatula, gently fold in Cool Whip™. Place mixture in a freezer safe container and freeze for at least 24 hours prior to serving.

- Remove from freezer and uncover at least 45 minutes (30 minutes small batch) prior to serving if you want to enjoy using a straw. If using spoons, ice cream can be enjoyed immediately.

> **Garnish Ideas:** Whipped Cream, Chocolate Syrup, Chocolate Shavings, Coconut & Chocolate Cookies

CHOCOLATE SCOTCH-A-ROO

Ingredients

Large Batch

- 1 Gallon Chocolate Ice Cream
- 16 oz. Cool Whip™
- 1 Cup Butterscotch Schnapps
- 1 Cup Caramel Vodka

Small Batch

- 2 Cups Chocolate Ice Cream
- ½ Cup Cool Whip™
- 1 oz. Butterscotch Schnapps
- 1 oz. Caramel Vodka

Instructions

- Remove ice cream and Cool Whip™ from freezer ahead of time. Cool Whip™ should be completely thawed before using. Ice cream should be soft enough to mix with an electric hand mixer. In an extra large mixing bowl, blend ice cream until smooth. Combine butterscotch schnapps and caramel vodka with ice cream and mix until fully blended. Using a spatula, gently fold in Cool Whip™. Place mixture in a freezer safe container and freeze for at least 24 hours prior to serving.

- Remove from freezer and uncover at least 45 minutes (30 minutes small batch) prior to serving if you want to enjoy using a straw. If using spoons, ice cream can be enjoyed immediately.

> **Garnish Ideas:** Whipped Cream, Butterscotch Syrup, Caramel Syrup, Chocolate Shavings & Butterscotch Chips

Fruity Delights

Blueberry Bombs

BLUEBERRY BOMBS

Ingredients

Large Batch	Small Batch
1 Gallon Vanilla Ice Cream	2 Cups Vanilla Ice Cream
16 oz. Cool Whip™	½ Cup Cool Whip™
1 ½ Cups Blueberry Liqueur	1 ½ oz. Blueberry Liqueur
1 Cup White Chocolate Liqueur	1 oz. White Chocolate Liqueur
Blue Food Coloring – To Desired Color	Blue Food Coloring - To Desired Color

Instructions

- Remove ice cream and Cool Whip™ from freezer ahead of time. Cool Whip™ should be completely thawed before using. Ice cream should be soft enough to mix with an electric hand mixer. In an extra large mixing bowl, blend ice cream until smooth. Combine blueberry liqueur, white chocolate liqueur and food coloring with ice cream and mix until fully blended. Using a spatula, gently fold in Cool Whip™. Place mixture in a freezer safe container and freeze for at least 24 hours prior to serving.

- Remove from freezer and uncover at least 45 minutes (30 minutes small batch) prior to serving if you want to enjoy using a straw. If using spoons, ice cream can be enjoyed immediately.

> **Garnish Ideas:** Whipped Cream, Vanilla Sugar Wafer Cookies & Blueberries

YES, I LIKE PINA COLADAS

Ingredients

Large Batch	Small Batch
1 Gallon Vanilla Ice Cream	2 Cups Vanilla Ice Cream
16 oz. Cool Whip™	½ Cup Cool Whip™
1 ½ Cups Coconut Rum	1 ½ oz. Coconut Rum
1 Cup Pineapple Rum	1 oz. Pineapple Rum

Instructions

- Remove ice cream and Cool Whip™ from freezer ahead of time. Cool Whip™ should be completely thawed before using. Ice cream should be soft enough to mix with an electric hand mixer. In an extra large mixing bowl, blend ice cream until smooth. Combine coconut rum and pineapple rum with ice cream and mix until fully blended. Using a spatula, gently fold in Cool Whip™. Place mixture in a freezer safe container and freeze for at least 24 hours prior to serving.

- Remove from freezer and uncover at least 45 minutes (30 minutes small batch) prior to serving if you want to enjoy using a straw. If using spoons, ice cream can be enjoyed immediately.

Garnish Ideas: Whipped Cream, Vanilla Sugar Wafer Cookies & Assorted Fruit

STRAWBERRY SENSATIONS

Ingredients

Large Batch	Small Batch
1 Gallon Vanilla Ice Cream	2 Cups Vanilla Ice Cream
16 oz. Cool Whip™	½ Cup Cool Whip™
1 Cup Strawberry Rum	1 oz. Strawberry Rum
1 Cup Tequila Rose™	1 oz. Tequila Rose™
Red Food Coloring – To Desired Color	Red Food Coloring - To Desired Color

Instructions

- Remove ice cream and Cool Whip™ from freezer ahead of time. Cool Whip™ should be completely thawed before using. Ice cream should be soft enough to mix with an electric hand mixer. In an extra large mixing bowl, blend ice cream until smooth. Combine strawberry rum, Tequila Rose™ and red food coloring with ice cream and mix until fully blended. Using a spatula, gently fold in Cool Whip™. Place mixture in a freezer safe container and freeze for at least 24 hours prior to serving.

- Remove from freezer and uncover at least 45 minutes (30 minutes small batch) prior to serving if you want to enjoy using a straw. If using spoons, ice cream can be enjoyed immediately.

> **Garnish Ideas:** Whipped Cream, Vanilla Sugar Wafer Cookies, Strawberry Gummies & Fresh Strawberries

PEACHES & CREAM TANGO

Ingredients

Large Batch	Small Batch
1 Gallon Vanilla Ice Cream	2 Cups Vanilla Ice Cream
16 oz. Cool Whip™	½ Cup Cool Whip™
1 Cup Peach Schnapps	1 oz. Peach Schnapps
1 Cup Peach Liqueur	1 oz. Peach Liqueur
Red & Yellow Food Coloring – To Desired Level	Red & Yellow Food Coloring – To Desired Level

Instructions

- Remove ice cream and Cool Whip™ from freezer ahead of time. Cool Whip™ should be completely thawed before using. Ice cream should be soft enough to mix with an electric hand mixer. In an extra large mixing bowl, blend ice cream until smooth. Combine peach schnapps, peach liqueur and food coloring with ice cream and mix until fully blended. Using a spatula, gently fold in Cool Whip™. Place mixture in a freezer safe container and freeze for at least 24 hours prior to serving.

- Remove from freezer and uncover at least 45 minutes (30 minutes small batch) prior to serving if you want to enjoy using a straw. If using spoons, ice cream can be enjoyed immediately.

Garnish Ideas: Whipped Cream, Vanilla Sugar Wafer Cookies & Peach Slices

TRIPLE BERRY BLISS

Ingredients

Large Batch	Small Batch
1 Gallon Strawberry Ice Cream	2 Cups Strawberry Ice Cream
16 oz. Cool Whip™	½ Cup Cool Whip™
1 Cup Blackberry Brandy	1 oz. Blackberry Brandy
1 Cup Raspberry Liqueur	1 oz. Raspberry Liqueur

Instructions

- Remove ice cream and Cool Whip™ from freezer ahead of time. Cool Whip™ should be completely thawed before using. Ice cream should be soft enough to mix with an electric hand mixer. In an extra large mixing bowl, blend ice cream until smooth. Combine blackberry brandy and raspberry liqueur with ice cream and mix until fully blended. Using a spatula, gently fold in Cool Whip™. Place mixture in a freezer safe container and freeze for at least 24 hours prior to serving.

- Remove from freezer and uncover at least 45 minutes (30 minutes small batch) prior to serving if you want to enjoy using a straw. If using spoons, ice cream can be enjoyed immediately.

> **Garnish Ideas:** Whipped Cream, White Chocolate Shavings, Vanilla Cookies & Assorted Berries

GROOVY CHOCOLATE STRAWBERRY

Ingredients

Large Batch	Small Batch
1 Gallon Strawberry Ice Cream	2 Cups Strawberry Ice Cream
16 oz. Cool Whip™	½ Cup Cool Whip™
1 Cup Strawberry Rum	1 oz. Strawberry Rum
1 Cup White Chocolate Liqueur	1 oz. White Chocolate Liqueur

Instructions

- Remove ice cream and Cool Whip™ from freezer ahead of time. Cool Whip™ should be completely thawed before using. Ice cream should be soft enough to mix with an electric hand mixer. In an extra large mixing bowl, blend ice cream until smooth. Combine strawberry rum and white chocolate liqueur with ice cream and mix until fully blended. Using a spatula, gently fold in Cool Whip™. Place mixture in a freezer safe container and freeze for at least 24 hours prior to serving.

- Remove from freezer and uncover at least 45 minutes (30 minutes small batch) prior to serving if you want to enjoy using a straw. If using spoons, ice cream can be enjoyed immediately.

> **Garnish Ideas:** Whipped Cream, Chocolate Syrup, Chocolate Shavings & Strawberries

APPLE CINNAMON TURNOVER

Ingredients

Large Batch	Small Batch
1 Gallon Vanilla Ice Cream	2 Cups Vanilla Ice Cream
16 oz. Cool Whip™	½ Cup Cool Whip™
1 ½ Cups Apple Schnapps	1 ½ oz. Apple Schnapps
¼ Cup Cinnamon Liqueur	2 Tsp. Cinnamon Liqueur

Instructions

- Remove ice cream and Cool Whip™ from freezer ahead of time. Cool Whip™ should be completely thawed before using. Ice cream should be soft enough to mix with an electric hand mixer. In an extra large mixing bowl, blend ice cream until smooth. Combine apple schnapps and cinnamon liqueur with ice cream and mix until fully blended. Using a spatula, gently fold in Cool Whip™. Place mixture in a freezer safe container and freeze for at least 24 hours prior to serving.

- Remove from freezer and uncover at least 45 minutes (30 minutes small batch) prior to serving if you want to enjoy using a straw. If using spoons, ice cream can be enjoyed immediately.

> **Garnish Ideas:** Whipped Cream, Ground Cinnamon & Apple Slices

THE SALTY PIRATE

Ingredients

Large Batch	Small Batch
1 Gallon Vanilla Ice Cream	2 Cups Vanilla Ice Cream
16 oz. Cool Whip™	½ Cup Cool Whip™
1 Cup Coconut Rum	1 oz. Coconut Rum
1 Cup Salted Caramel Irish Cream	1 oz. Salted Caramel Irish Cream

Instructions

▪ Remove ice cream and Cool Whip™ from freezer ahead of time. Cool Whip™ should be completely thawed before using. Ice cream should be soft enough to mix with an electric hand mixer. In an extra large mixing bowl, blend ice cream until smooth. Combine coconut rum and salted caramel Irish cream with ice cream and mix until fully blended. Using a spatula, gently fold in Cool Whip™. Place mixture in a freezer safe container and freeze for at least 24 hours prior to serving.

▪ Remove from freezer and uncover at least 45 minutes (30 minutes small batch) prior to serving if you want to enjoy using a straw. If using spoons, ice cream can be enjoyed immediately.

Garnish Ideas: Whipped Cream, Chocolate Shavings, Coconut Shavings, Caramel Syrup & Maraschino Cherries

CHERRY COLA FLOAT

Ingredients

Large Batch	Small Batch
1 Gallon Vanilla Ice Cream	2 Cups Vanilla Ice Cream
16 oz. Cool Whip™	½ Cup Cool Whip™
1 Cup Cola Rum	1 oz. Cola Rum
1 Cup Black Cherry Rum	1 oz. Black Cherry Rum

Instructions

- Remove ice cream and Cool Whip™ from freezer ahead of time. Cool Whip™ should be completely thawed before using. Ice cream should be soft enough to mix with an electric hand mixer. In an extra large mixing bowl, blend ice cream until smooth. Combine cola rum and black cherry rum with ice cream and mix until fully blended. Using a spatula, gently fold in Cool Whip™. Place mixture in a freezer safe container and freeze for at least 24 hours prior to serving.

- Remove from freezer and uncover at least 45 minutes (30 minutes small batch) prior to serving if you want to enjoy using a straw. If using spoons, ice cream can be enjoyed immediately.

> **Garnish Ideas:** Whipped Cream & Maraschino Cherries

LEMON MERINGUE PIE

Ingredients

Large Batch	Small Batch
1 Gallon Vanilla Ice Cream	2 Cups Vanilla Ice Cream
16 oz. Cool Whip™	½ Cup Cool Whip™
1 Cup Limoncello	1 oz. Limoncello
1 Cup Whipped Cream Vodka	1 oz. Whipped Cream Vodka
Yellow Food Coloring – To Desired Level	Yellow Food Coloring – To Desired Level

Instructions

- Remove ice cream and Cool Whip™ from freezer ahead of time. Cool Whip™ should be completely thawed before using. Ice cream should be soft enough to mix with an electric hand mixer. In an extra large mixing bowl, blend ice cream until smooth. Combine limoncello, whipped cream vodka and food coloring with ice cream and mix until fully blended. Using a spatula, gently fold in Cool Whip™. Place mixture in a freezer safe container and freeze for at least 24 hours prior to serving.

- Remove from freezer and uncover at least 45 minutes (30 minutes small batch) prior to serving if you want to enjoy using a straw. If using spoons, ice cream can be enjoyed immediately.

Garnish Ideas: Whipped Cream, Maraschino Cherries, Lemon Cookies, Graham Crackers & Candied Lemon Slices

FRUITY HURRICANES

Ingredients

Large Batch	Small Batch
1 Gallon Vanilla Ice Cream	2 Cups Vanilla Ice Cream
16 oz. Cool Whip™	½ Cup Cool Whip™
1 Cup Triple Sec	1 oz. Triple Sec
1/2 Cup Pineapple Rum	½ oz. Pineapple Rum
1/2 Cup Maraschino Liqueur	½ oz. Maraschino Liqueur

Instructions

▪ Remove ice cream and Cool Whip™ from freezer ahead of time. Cool Whip™ should be completely thawed before using. Ice cream should be soft enough to mix with an electric hand mixer. In an extra large mixing bowl, blend ice cream until smooth. Combine triple sec, pineapple rum and maraschino liqueur with ice cream and mix until fully blended. Using a spatula, gently fold in Cool Whip™. Place mixture in a freezer safe container and freeze for at least 24 hours prior to serving.

▪ Remove from freezer and uncover at least 45 minutes (30 minutes small batch) prior to serving if you want to enjoy using a straw. If using spoons, ice cream can be enjoyed immediately.

Garnish Ideas: Whipped Cream, Maraschino Cherries & Assorted Fruit

LIQUID BANANA SPLIT

Ingredients

Large Batch	Small Batch
1 Gallon Neapolitan Ice Cream	2 Cups Neapolitan Ice Cream
16 oz. Cool Whip™	½ Cup Cool Whip™
1 Cup White Chocolate Liqueur	1 oz. White Chocolate Liqueur
1 Cup Strawberry Vodka	1 oz. Strawberry Vodka
1 Cup Banana Liqueur	1 oz. Banana Liqueur

Instructions

- Remove ice cream and Cool Whip™ from freezer ahead of time. Cool Whip™ should be completely thawed before using. Ice cream should be soft enough to mix with an electric hand mixer. In an extra large mixing bowl, blend ice cream until smooth. Combine white chocolate liqueur, strawberry vodka and banana liqueur with ice cream and mix until fully blended. Using a spatula, gently fold in Cool Whip™. Place mixture in a freezer safe container and freeze for at least 24 hours prior to serving.

- Remove from freezer and uncover at least 45 minutes (30 minutes small batch) prior to serving if you want to enjoy using a straw. If using spoons, ice cream can be enjoyed immediately.

Garnish Ideas: Whipped Cream, Banana Slices, Chocolate Syrup, Chocolate Shavings & Maraschino Cherries

CHOCOLATE COVERED CHERRY

Ingredients

Large Batch	Small Batch
1 Gallon Cherry Chunk Ice Cream	2 Cups Cherry Chunk Ice Cream
16 oz. Cool Whip™	½ Cup Cool Whip™
1 Cup Chocolate Liqueur	1 oz. Chocolate Liqueur
1 Cup Black Cherry Rum	1 oz. Black Cherry Rum

Instructions

- Remove ice cream and Cool Whip™ from freezer ahead of time. Cool Whip™ should be completely thawed before using. Ice cream should be soft enough to mix with an electric hand mixer. In an extra large mixing bowl, blend ice cream until smooth. Combine chocolate liqueur and black cherry rum with ice cream and mix until fully blended. Using a spatula, gently fold in Cool Whip™. Place mixture in a freezer safe container and freeze for at least 24 hours prior to serving.

- Remove from freezer and uncover at least 45 minutes (30 minutes small batch) prior to serving if you want to enjoy using a straw. If using spoons, ice cream can be enjoyed immediately.

> **Garnish Ideas:** Whipped Cream, Chocolate Syrup, Chocolate Shavings & Maraschino Cherries

FROZEN CARMEL APPLE

Ingredients

Large Batch	Small Batch
1 Gallon Vanilla Ice Cream	2 Cups Vanilla Ice Cream
16 oz. Cool Whip™	½ Cup Cool Whip™
1 Cup Apple Schnapps	1 oz. Apple Schnapps
1 Cup Caramel Liqueur	1 oz. Caramel Liqueur

Instructions

- Remove ice cream and Cool Whip™ from freezer ahead of time. Cool Whip™ should be completely thawed before using. Ice cream should be soft enough to mix with an electric hand mixer. In an extra large mixing bowl, blend ice cream until smooth. Combine apple schnapps and caramel liqueur with ice cream and mix until fully blended. Using a spatula, gently fold in Cool Whip™. Place mixture in a freezer safe container and freeze for at least 24 hours prior to serving.

- Remove from freezer and uncover at least 45 minutes (30 minutes small batch) prior to serving if you want to enjoy using a straw. If using spoons, ice cream can be enjoyed immediately.

> **Garnish Ideas:** Whipped Cream, Caramel Syrup & Apple Slices

SECTION 3

Delicious Indulgences

Cookies 'N' Cream Grasshoppers

COOKIES 'N' CREAM GRASSHOPPERS

Ingredients

Large Batch	Small Batch
1 Gallon Cookies 'N' Cream Ice Cream	2 Cups Cookies 'N' Cream Ice Cream
16 oz. Cool Whip™	½ Cup Cool Whip™
1 Cup Crème de Menthe	1 oz. Crème de Menthe
1 Cup Crème de Cacao	1 oz. Crème de Cacao

Instructions

- Remove ice cream and Cool Whip™ from freezer ahead of time. Cool Whip™ should be completely thawed before using. Ice cream should be soft enough to mix with an electric hand mixer. In an extra large mixing bowl, blend ice cream until smooth. Combine crème de menthe and crème de cacao with ice cream and mix until fully blended. Using a spatula, gently fold in Cool Whip™. Place mixture in a freezer safe container and freeze for at least 24 hours prior to serving.

- Remove from freezer and uncover at least 45 minutes (30 minutes small batch) prior to serving if you want to enjoy using a straw. If using spoons, ice cream can be enjoyed immediately.

> **Garnish Ideas:** Whipped Cream, Chocolate Mint Candies, Maraschino Cherries & Mint Cookies

ICY VANILLA CINNAMON

Ingredients

Large Batch	Small Batch
1 Gallon Vanilla Ice Cream	2 Cups Vanilla Ice Cream
16 oz. Cool Whip™	½ Cup Cool Whip™
1 Cup Fireball Whiskey™	1 oz. Fireball Whiskey™

Instructions

- Remove ice cream and Cool Whip™ from freezer ahead of time. Cool Whip™ should be completely thawed before using. Ice cream should be soft enough to mix with an electric hand mixer. In an extra large mixing bowl, blend ice cream until smooth. Combine Fireball Whiskey™ with ice cream and mix until fully blended. Using a spatula, gently fold in Cool Whip™. Place mixture in a freezer safe container and freeze for at least 24 hours prior to serving.

- Remove from freezer and uncover at least 45 minutes (30 minutes small batch) prior to serving if you want to enjoy using a straw. If using spoons, ice cream can be enjoyed immediately.

> **Garnish Ideas:** Whipped Cream, Brown Sugar, Ground Cinnamon & Vanilla Sugar Wafer Cookies

FROSTY CAPPUCCINO

Ingredients

Large Batch	Small Batch
1 Gallon Chocolate Ice Cream	2 Cups Chocolate Ice Cream
16 oz. Cool Whip™	½ Cup Cool Whip™
1 Cup RumChata™	1 oz. RumChata™
1 Cup Espresso Liqueur	1 oz. Espresso Liqueur

Instructions

- Remove ice cream and Cool Whip™ from freezer ahead of time. Cool Whip™ should be completely thawed before using. Ice cream should be soft enough to mix with an electric hand mixer. In an extra large mixing bowl, blend ice cream until smooth. Combine RumChata™ and espresso liqueur with ice cream and mix until fully blended. Using a spatula, gently fold in Cool Whip™. Place mixture in a freezer safe container and freeze for at least 24 hours prior to serving.

- Remove from freezer and uncover at least 45 minutes (30 minutes small batch) prior to serving if you want to enjoy using a straw. If using spoons, ice cream can be enjoyed immediately.

Garnish Ideas: Whipped Cream, Cocoa Powder, Chocolate Syrup & Chocolate Wafer Cookies

HAPPY BIRTHDAY TO ME!

Ingredients

Large Batch	Small Batch
1 Gallon Vanilla Ice Cream	2 Cups Vanilla Ice Cream
16 oz. Cool Whip™	½ Cup Cool Whip™
1 Cup Cake Vodka	1 oz. Cake Vodka
1 Cup White Chocolate Liqueur	1 oz. White Chocolate Liqueur

Instructions

- Remove ice cream and Cool Whip™ from freezer ahead of time. Cool Whip™ should be completely thawed before using. Ice cream should be soft enough to mix with an electric hand mixer. In an extra large mixing bowl, blend ice cream until smooth. Combine cake vodka and white chocolate liqueur with ice cream and mix until fully blended. Using a spatula, gently fold in Cool Whip™. Place mixture in a freezer safe container and freeze for at least 24 hours prior to serving.

- Remove from freezer and uncover at least 45 minutes (30 minutes small batch) prior to serving if you want to enjoy using a straw. If using spoons, ice cream can be enjoyed immediately.

> **Garnish Ideas:** Whipped Cream & Sprinkles

HAPPY
BIRTHDAY
TO ME!

GINGER SNAP FREEZE

Ingredients

Large Batch	Small Batch
1 Gallon Vanilla Ice Cream	2 Cups Vanilla Ice Cream
16 oz. Cool Whip™	½ Cup Cool Whip™
1 ½ Cups Ginger Vodka	1 ½ oz. Ginger Vodka
2 Tsp. Ground Cinnamon	¼ Tsp. Ground Cinnamon

Instructions

- Remove ice cream and Cool Whip™ from freezer ahead of time. Cool Whip™ should be completely thawed before using. Ice cream should be soft enough to mix with an electric hand mixer. In an extra large mixing bowl, blend ice cream until smooth. Combine ginger vodka and ground cinnamon with ice cream and mix until fully blended. Using a spatula, gently fold in Cool Whip™. Place mixture in a freezer safe container and freeze for at least 24 hours prior to serving.

- Remove from freezer and uncover at least 45 minutes (30 minutes small batch) prior to serving if you want to enjoy using a straw. If using spoons, ice cream can be enjoyed immediately.

Garnish Ideas: Whipped Cream, Caramel Syrup, Ground Cinnamon & Ginger Cookies

SUNKEN ROOT BEER BARREL

Ingredients

Large Batch	Small Batch
1 Gallon Vanilla Ice Cream	2 Cups Vanilla Ice Cream
16 oz. Cool Whip™	½ Cup Cool Whip™
1 ½ Cups Root Beer Schnapps	1 ½ oz. Root Beer Schnapps

Instructions

- Remove ice cream and Cool Whip™ from freezer ahead of time. Cool Whip™ should be completely thawed before using. Ice cream should be soft enough to mix with an electric hand mixer. In an extra large mixing bowl, blend ice cream until smooth. Combine root beer schnapps with ice cream and mix until fully blended. Using a spatula, gently fold in Cool Whip™. Place mixture in a freezer safe container and freeze for at least 24 hours prior to serving.

- Remove from freezer and uncover at least 45 minutes (30 minutes small batch) prior to serving if you want to enjoy using a straw. If using spoons, ice cream can be enjoyed immediately.

Garnish Ideas: Whipped Cream, Maraschino Cherries & Vanilla Sugar Wafer Cookies

WHITE CHOCOLATE RASPBERRY

Ingredients

Large Batch	Small Batch
1 Gallon Vanilla Ice Cream	2 Cups Vanilla Ice Cream
16 oz. Cool Whip™	½ Cup Cool Whip™
1 Cup White Chocolate Liqueur	1 oz. White Chocolate Liqueur
1 Cup Raspberry Liqueur	1 oz. Raspberry Liqueur

Instructions

- Remove ice cream and Cool Whip™ from freezer ahead of time. Cool Whip™ should be completely thawed before using. Ice cream should be soft enough to mix with an electric hand mixer. In an extra large mixing bowl, blend ice cream until smooth. Combine white chocolate liqueur and raspberry liqueur with ice cream and mix until fully blended. Using a spatula, gently fold in Cool Whip™. Place mixture in a freezer safe container and freeze for at least 24 hours prior to serving.

- Remove from freezer and uncover at least 45 minutes (30 minutes small batch) prior to serving if you want to enjoy using a straw. If using spoons, ice cream can be enjoyed immediately.

Garnish Ideas: Whipped Cream, White Chocolate Candies & Raspberries

ADULT OREO™ OVERLOAD

Ingredients

Large Batch

1 Gallon Cookies 'N' Cream Ice Cream
16 oz. Cool Whip™
1 Cup White Chocolate Liqueur
1 Cup Whipped Cream Vodka

Small Batch

2 Cups Cookies 'N' Cream Ice Cream
½ Cup Cool Whip™
1 oz. White Chocolate Liqueur
1 oz. Whipped Cream Vodka

Instructions

- Remove ice cream and Cool Whip™ from freezer ahead of time. Cool Whip™ should be completely thawed before using. Ice cream should be soft enough to mix with an electric hand mixer. In an extra large mixing bowl, blend ice cream until smooth. Combine white chocolate liqueur and whipped cream vodka with ice cream and mix until fully blended. Using a spatula, gently fold in Cool Whip™. Place mixture in a freezer safe container and freeze for at least 24 hours prior to serving.

- Remove from freezer and uncover at least 45 minutes (30 minutes small batch) prior to serving if you want to enjoy using a straw. If using spoons, ice cream can be enjoyed immediately.

> **Garnish Ideas:** Whipped Cream, Maraschino Cherries & Oreo™ Cookies

VANILLA BEAN SWIRL

Ingredients

Large Batch	Small Batch
1 Gallon Vanilla Bean Ice Cream	2 Cups Vanilla Bean Ice Cream
16 oz. Cool Whip™	½ Cup Cool Whip™
1 Cup Vanilla Rum	1 oz. Vanilla Rum
1 Cup Vanilla Vodka	1 oz. Vanilla Vodka

Instructions

- Remove ice cream and Cool Whip™ from freezer ahead of time. Cool Whip™ should be completely thawed before using. Ice cream should be soft enough to mix with an electric hand mixer. In an extra large mixing bowl, blend ice cream until smooth. Combine vanilla rum and vanilla vodka with ice cream and mix until fully blended. Using a spatula, gently fold in Cool Whip™. Place mixture in a freezer safe container and freeze for at least 24 hours prior to serving.

- Remove from freezer and uncover at least 45 minutes (30 minutes small batch) prior to serving if you want to enjoy using a straw. If using spoons, ice cream can be enjoyed immediately.

> **Garnish Ideas:** Whipped Cream, Maraschino Cherries & Vanilla Wafer Cookies

JIVING JAVA

Ingredients

Large Batch	Small Batch
1 Gallon Vanilla Ice Cream	2 Cups Vanilla Ice Cream
16 oz. Cool Whip™	½ Cup Cool Whip™
1 Cup Kahlua™	1 oz. Kahlua™
1 Cup Espresso Liqueur	1 oz. Espresso Liqueur

Instructions

- Remove ice cream and Cool Whip™ from freezer ahead of time. Cool Whip™ should be completely thawed before using. Ice cream should be soft enough to mix with an electric hand mixer. In an extra large mixing bowl, blend ice cream until smooth. Combine Kahlua™ and espresso liqueur with ice cream and mix until fully blended. Using a spatula, gently fold in Cool Whip™. Place mixture in a freezer safe container and freeze for at least 24 hours prior to serving.

- Remove from freezer and uncover at least 45 minutes (30 minutes small batch) prior to serving if you want to enjoy using a straw. If using spoons, ice cream can be enjoyed immediately.

> **Garnish Ideas:** Whipped Cream, Cocoa Powder, Chocolate Syrup & Wafer Cookies

Ice Cream Under The Influence

CHOCOLATE RUMCHATA™

Ingredients

Large Batch	Small Batch
1 Gallon Chocolate Ice Cream	2 Cups Chocolate Ice Cream
16 oz. Cool Whip™	½ Cup Cool Whip™
1 Cup RumChata™	1 oz. RumChata™
1 Cup Chocolate Liqueur	1 oz. Chocolate Liqueur

Instructions

- Remove ice cream and Cool Whip™ from freezer ahead of time. Cool Whip™ should be completely thawed before using. Ice cream should be soft enough to mix with an electric hand mixer. In an extra large mixing bowl, blend ice cream until smooth. Combine RumChata™ and chocolate liqueur with ice cream and mix until fully blended. Using a spatula, gently fold in Cool Whip™. Place mixture in a freezer safe container and freeze for at least 24 hours prior to serving.

- Remove from freezer and uncover at least 45 minutes (30 minutes small batch) prior to serving if you want to enjoy using a straw. If using spoons, ice cream can be enjoyed immediately.

> **Garnish Ideas:** Whipped Cream, Chocolate Syrup & Chocolate or Vanilla Cookies

WHITE CHOCOLATE MACADAMIA NUT

Ingredients

Large Batch	Small Batch
1 Gallon Vanilla Ice Cream	2 Cups Vanilla Ice Cream
16 oz. Cool Whip™	½ Cup Cool Whip™
1 Cup Macadamia Nut Liqueur	1 oz. Macadamia Nut Liqueur
1 Cup White Chocolate Liqueur	1 oz. White Chocolate Liqueur

Instructions

- Remove ice cream and Cool Whip™ from freezer ahead of time. Cool Whip™ should be completely thawed before using. Ice cream should be soft enough to mix with an electric hand mixer. In an extra large mixing bowl, blend ice cream until smooth. Combine macadamia nut liqueur and white chocolate liqueur with ice cream and mix until fully blended. Using a spatula, gently fold in Cool Whip™. Place mixture in a freezer safe container and freeze for at least 24 hours prior to serving.

- Remove from freezer and uncover at least 45 minutes (30 minutes small batch) prior to serving if you want to enjoy using a straw. If using spoons, ice cream can be enjoyed immediately.

> **Garnish Ideas:** Whipped Cream, Caramel Syrup, Vanilla Cookies & Macadamia Nuts

IRISH CREAM ICE CREAM DREAM

Ingredients

Large Batch	Small Batch
1 Gallon Vanilla Ice Cream	2 Cups Vanilla Ice Cream
16 oz. Cool Whip™	½ Cup Cool Whip™
2 Cups Irish Cream	2 oz. Irish Cream
1 Cup Chocolate Liqueur	1 oz. Chocolate Liqueur

Instructions

- Remove ice cream and Cool Whip™ from freezer ahead of time. Cool Whip™ should be completely thawed before using. Ice cream should be soft enough to mix with an electric hand mixer. In an extra large mixing bowl, blend ice cream until smooth. Combine Irish cream and chocolate liqueur with ice cream and mix until fully blended. Using a spatula, gently fold in Cool Whip™. Place mixture in a freezer safe container and freeze for at least 24 hours prior to serving.

- Remove from freezer and uncover at least 45 minutes (30 minutes small batch) prior to serving if you want to enjoy using a straw. If using spoons, ice cream can be enjoyed immediately.

Garnish Ideas: Whipped Cream, Chocolate Syrup, Chocolate Shavings & Fudge Sticks

FROZEN S'MORES

Ingredients

Large Batch	Small Batch
1 Gallon Vanilla Ice Cream	2 Cups Vanilla Ice Cream
16 oz. Cool Whip™	½ Cup Cool Whip™
1 Cup Marshmallow Liqueur	1 oz. Marshmallow Liqueur
1 Cup Dark Chocolate Liqueur	1 oz. Dark Chocolate Liqueur
½ Cup Honey Whiskey	½ oz. Honey Whiskey

Instructions

- Remove ice cream and Cool Whip™ from freezer ahead of time. Cool Whip™ should be completely thawed before using. Ice cream should be soft enough to mix with an electric hand mixer. In an extra large mixing bowl, blend ice cream until smooth. Combine marshmallow liqueur, dark chocolate liqueur and honey whiskey with ice cream and mix until fully blended. Using a spatula, gently fold in Cool Whip™. Place mixture in a freezer safe container and freeze for at least 24 hours prior to serving.

- Remove from freezer and uncover at least 45 minutes (30 minutes small batch) prior to serving if you want to enjoy using a straw. If using spoons, ice cream can be enjoyed immediately.

> **Garnish Ideas:** Whipped Cream, Chocolate Candy Bar Pieces, Graham Crackers & Mini Marshmallows

Drinks For Everyone

(Alcohol-Free Versions)

Chocolate Almond Happiness

CHOCOLATE ALMOND HAPPINESS

Ingredients

Large Batch	Small Batch
1 Gallon Chocolate Ice Cream	2 Cups Chocolate Ice Cream
16 oz. Cool Whip™	½ Cup Cool Whip™
4 Tbs. Almond Extract	2 Tsp. Almond Extract

Instructions

- Remove ice cream and Cool Whip™ from freezer ahead of time. Cool Whip™ should be completely thawed before using. Ice cream should be soft enough to mix with an electric hand mixer. In an extra large mixing bowl, blend ice cream until smooth. Combine almond extract with ice cream and mix until fully blended. Using a spatula, gently fold in Cool Whip™. Place mixture in a freezer safe container and freeze for at least 24 hours prior to serving.

- Remove from freezer and uncover at least 45 minutes (30 minutes small batch) prior to serving if you want to enjoy using a straw. If using spoons, ice cream can be enjoyed immediately.

> **Garnish Ideas:** Whipped Cream, Chocolate Syrup, Chocolate Shavings & Chocolate Covered Almonds

LET'S GO BANANAS

Ingredients

Large Batch	Small Batch
1 Gallon Chocolate Ice Cream	2 Cups Chocolate Ice Cream
16 oz. Cool Whip™	½ Cup Cool Whip™
1 ½ Tbs. Banana Extract	½ Tsp. Banana Extract

Instructions

▪ Remove ice cream and Cool Whip™ from freezer ahead of time. Cool Whip™ should be completely thawed before using. Ice cream should be soft enough to mix with an electric hand mixer. In an extra large mixing bowl, blend ice cream until smooth. Combine banana extract with ice cream and mix until fully blended. Using a spatula, gently fold in Cool Whip™. Place mixture in a freezer safe container and freeze for at least 24 hours prior to serving.

▪ Remove from freezer and uncover at least 45 minutes (30 minutes small batch) prior to serving if you want to enjoy using a straw. If using spoons, ice cream can be enjoyed immediately.

> **Garnish Ideas:** Whipped Cream, Dark Chocolate Syrup, Chocolate Shavings, Chocolate Cookies & Coconut Shavings

DARK CHOCOLATE COCONUT

Ingredients

Large Batch	Small Batch
1 Gallon Chocolate Ice Cream	2 Cups Chocolate Ice Cream
16 oz. Cool Whip™	½ Cup Cool Whip™
1 ½ Tbs. Coconut Extract	½ Tsp. Coconut Extract
½ Cup Dark Chocolate Syrup	1 Tbs. Dark Chocolate Syrup

Instructions

- Remove ice cream and Cool Whip™ from freezer ahead of time. Cool Whip™ should be completely thawed before using. Ice cream should be soft enough to mix with an electric hand mixer. In an extra large mixing bowl, blend ice cream until smooth. Combine coconut extract and dark chocolate syrup with ice cream and mix until fully blended. Using a spatula, gently fold in Cool Whip™. Place mixture in a freezer safe container and freeze for at least 24 hours prior to serving.

- Remove from freezer and uncover at least 45 minutes (30 minutes small batch) prior to serving if you want to enjoy using a straw. If using spoons, ice cream can be enjoyed immediately.

Garnish Ideas: Whipped Cream, Dark Chocolate Syrup, Chocolate Shavings, Chocolate Cookies & Coconut Shavings

FRIGID TURTLES

Ingredients

Large Batch	Small Batch
1 Gallon Butter Pecan Ice Cream	2 Cups Butter Pecan Ice Cream
16 oz. Cool Whip™	½ Cup Cool Whip™
½ Cup Carmel Syrup	1 Tbs. Carmel Syrup
½ Cup Chocolate Syrup	1 Tbs. Chocolate Syrup

Instructions

- Remove ice cream and Cool Whip™ from freezer ahead of time. Cool Whip™ should be completely thawed before using. Ice cream should be soft enough to mix with an electric hand mixer. In an extra large mixing bowl, blend ice cream until smooth. Combine caramel syrup and chocolate syrup with ice cream and mix until fully blended. Using a spatula, gently fold in Cool Whip™. Place mixture in a freezer safe container and freeze for at least 24 hours prior to serving.

- Remove from freezer and uncover at least 45 minutes (30 minutes small batch) prior to serving if you want to enjoy using a straw. If using spoons, ice cream can be enjoyed immediately.

> **Garnish Ideas:** Whipped Cream, Chocolate Syrup, Carmel Syrup, Maraschino Cherries & Pecans

CHOCOLATE SCOTCH-A-ROO

Ingredients

Large Batch	Small Batch
1 Gallon Chocolate Ice Cream	2 Cups Chocolate Ice Cream
16 oz. Cool Whip™	½ Cup Cool Whip™
1 Cup Butterscotch Syrup	2 Tbs. Butterscotch Syrup
½ Cup Caramel Syrup	1 Tbs. Caramel Syrup

Instructions

- Remove ice cream and Cool Whip™ from freezer ahead of time. Cool Whip™ should be completely thawed before using. Ice cream should be soft enough to mix with an electric hand mixer. In an extra large mixing bowl, blend ice cream until smooth. Combine butterscotch syrup and caramel syrup with ice cream and mix until fully blended. Using a spatula, gently fold in Cool Whip™. Place mixture in a freezer safe container and freeze for at least 24 hours prior to serving.

- Remove from freezer and uncover at least 45 minutes (30 minutes small batch) prior to serving if you want to enjoy using a straw. If using spoons, ice cream can be enjoyed immediately.

> **Garnish Ideas:** Whipped Cream, Butterscotch Syrup, Caramel Syrup, Chocolate Shavings & Butterscotch Chips

BLUEBERRY BOMBS

Ingredients

Large Batch	Small Batch
1 Gallon Vanilla Ice Cream	2 Cups Vanilla Ice Cream
16 oz. Cool Whip™	½ Cup Cool Whip™
1 ½ Tbs. Blueberry Extract	½ Tsp. Blueberry Extract

Instructions

- Remove ice cream and Cool Whip™ from freezer ahead of time. Cool Whip™ should be completely thawed before using. Ice cream should be soft enough to mix with an electric hand mixer. In an extra large mixing bowl, blend ice cream until smooth. Combine blueberry extract with ice cream and mix until fully blended. Using a spatula, gently fold in Cool Whip™. Place mixture in a freezer safe container and freeze for at least 24 hours prior to serving.

- Remove from freezer and uncover at least 45 minutes (30 minutes small batch) prior to serving if you want to enjoy using a straw. If using spoons, ice cream can be enjoyed immediately.

> **Garnish Ideas:** Whipped Cream, Vanilla Sugar Wafer Cookies & Blueberries

STRAWBERRY SENSATIONS

Ingredients

Large Batch

1 Gallon Strawberry Ice Cream

16 oz. Cool Whip™

1 ½ Tbs. Strawberry Extract

½ Cup Strawberry Syrup

Small Batch

2 Cups Strawberry Ice Cream

½ Cup Cool Whip™

½ Tsp. Strawberry Extract

1 Tbs. Strawberry Syrup

Instructions

- Remove ice cream and Cool Whip™ from freezer ahead of time. Cool Whip™ should be completely thawed before using. Ice cream should be soft enough to mix with an electric hand mixer. In an extra large mixing bowl, blend ice cream until smooth. Combine strawberry extract and strawberry syrup with ice cream and mix until fully blended. Using a spatula, gently fold in Cool Whip™. Place mixture in a freezer safe container and freeze for at least 24 hours prior to serving.

- Remove from freezer and uncover at least 45 minutes (30 minutes small batch) prior to serving if you want to enjoy using a straw. If using spoons, ice cream can be enjoyed immediately.

> **Garnish Ideas:** Whipped Cream, Vanilla Sugar Wafer Cookies, Strawberry Gummies & Fresh Strawberries

TRIPLE BERRY BLISS

Ingredients

Large Batch	Small Batch
1 Gallon Strawberry Ice Cream	2 Cups Strawberry Ice Cream
16 oz. Cool Whip™	½ Cup Cool Whip™
1 Tbs. Raspberry Extract	½ Tsp. Raspberry Extract
1 Tbs. Blueberry Extract	½ Tsp. Blueberry Extract

Instructions

- Remove ice cream and Cool Whip™ from freezer ahead of time. Cool Whip™ should be completely thawed before using. Ice cream should be soft enough to mix with an electric hand mixer. In an extra large mixing bowl, blend ice cream until smooth. Combine raspberry and blueberry extract with ice cream and mix until fully blended. Using a spatula, gently fold in Cool Whip™. Place mixture in a freezer safe container and freeze for at least 24 hours prior to serving.

- Remove from freezer and uncover at least 45 minutes (30 minutes small batch) prior to serving if you want to enjoy using a straw. If using spoons, ice cream can be enjoyed immediately.

Garnish Ideas: Whipped Cream, White Chocolate Shavings, Vanilla Cookies & Assorted Berries

LEMON MERINGUE PIE

Ingredients

Large Batch	Small Batch
1 Gallon Vanilla Ice Cream	2 Cups Vanilla Ice Cream
24 oz. Cool Whip™	½ Cup Cool Whip™
2 ½ Tbs. Lemon Extract	1 Tsp. Lemon Extract
Yellow Food Coloring – To Desired Level	Yellow Food Coloring – To Desired Level

Instructions

- Remove ice cream and Cool Whip™ from freezer ahead of time. Cool Whip™ should be completely thawed before using. Ice cream should be soft enough to mix with an electric hand mixer. In an extra large mixing bowl, blend ice cream until smooth. Combine lemon extract and food coloring with ice cream and mix until fully blended. Using a spatula, gently fold in Cool Whip™. Place mixture in a freezer safe container and freeze for at least 24 hours prior to serving.

- Remove from freezer and uncover at least 45 minutes (30 minutes small batch) prior to serving if you want to enjoy using a straw. If using spoons, ice cream can be enjoyed immediately.

Garnish Ideas: Whipped Cream, Maraschino Cherries, Lemon Cookies, Graham Crackers & Candied Lemon Slices

LIQUID BANANA SPLIT

Ingredients

Large Batch	Small Batch
1 Gallon Neapolitan Ice Cream	2 Cups Neapolitan Ice Cream
16 oz. Cool Whip™	½ Cup Cool Whip™
1 ½ Tbs. Strawberry Extract	½ Tsp. Strawberry Extract
1 ½ Tbs. Banana Extract	½ Tsp. Banana Extract

Instructions

- Remove ice cream and Cool Whip™ from freezer ahead of time. Cool Whip™ should be completely thawed before using. Ice cream should be soft enough to mix with an electric hand mixer. In an extra large mixing bowl, blend ice cream until smooth. Combine strawberry extract and banana extract with ice cream and mix until fully blended. Using a spatula, gently fold in Cool Whip™. Place mixture in a freezer safe container and freeze for at least 24 hours prior to serving.

- Remove from freezer and uncover at least 45 minutes (30 minutes small batch) prior to serving if you want to enjoy using a straw. If using spoons, ice cream can be enjoyed immediately.

Garnish Ideas: Whipped Cream, Chocolate Syrup, Chocolate Shavings & Maraschino Cherries

CHOCOLATE COVERED CHERRY

Ingredients

Large Batch	Small Batch
1 Gallon Cherry Chunk Ice Cream	2 Cups Cherry Chunk Ice Cream
16 oz. Cool Whip™	½ Cup Cool Whip™
½ Cup Chocolate Syrup	1 Tbs. Chocolate Syrup
1 ½ Tbs. Cherry Extract	½ Tsp. Cherry Extract

Instructions

- Remove ice cream and Cool Whip™ from freezer ahead of time. Cool Whip™ should be completely thawed before using. Ice cream should be soft enough to mix with an electric hand mixer. In an extra large mixing bowl, blend ice cream until smooth. Combine chocolate syrup and cherry extract with ice cream and mix until fully blended. Using a spatula, gently fold in Cool Whip™. Place mixture in a freezer safe container and freeze for at least 24 hours prior to serving.

- Remove from freezer and uncover at least 45 minutes (30 minutes small batch) prior to serving if you want to enjoy using a straw. If using spoons, ice cream can be enjoyed immediately.

> **Garnish Ideas:** Whipped Cream, Chocolate Syrup, Chocolate Shavings & Maraschino Cherries

COOKIES 'N' CREAM GRASSHOPPERS

Ingredients

Large Batch	Small Batch
1 Gallon Cookies 'N' Cream Ice Cream	2 Cups Cookies 'N' Cream Ice Cream
16 oz. Cool Whip™	½ Cup Cool Whip™
½ Tbs. Mint Extract	½ Tsp. Mint Extract
½ Tsp. Green Food Coloring	Green Food Coloring - To Desired Color

Instructions

- Remove ice cream and Cool Whip™ from freezer ahead of time. Cool Whip™ should be completely thawed before using. Ice cream should be soft enough to mix with an electric hand mixer. In an extra large mixing bowl, blend ice cream until smooth. Combine mint extract and food coloring with ice cream and mix until fully blended. Using a spatula, gently fold in Cool Whip™. Place mixture in a freezer safe container and freeze for at least 24 hours prior to serving.

- Remove from freezer and uncover at least 45 minutes (30 minutes small batch) prior to serving if you want to enjoy using a straw. If using spoons, ice cream can be enjoyed immediately.

> **Garnish Ideas:** Whipped Cream, Chocolate Mint Candies, Maraschino Cherries & Mint Cookies

ICY VANILLA CINNAMON

Ingredients

Large Batch	Small Batch
1 Gallon Vanilla Ice Cream	2 Cups Vanilla Ice Cream
16 oz. Cool Whip™	½ Cup Cool Whip™
1 Tbs. Cinnamon Extract	½ Tsp. Cinnamon Extract
1 Tbs. Ground Cinnamon	½ Tsp. Ground Cinnamon

Instructions

- Remove ice cream and Cool Whip™ from freezer ahead of time. Cool Whip™ should be completely thawed before using. Ice cream should be soft enough to mix with an electric hand mixer. In an extra large mixing bowl, blend ice cream until smooth. Combine ground cinnamon and cinnamon extract with ice cream and mix until fully blended. Using a spatula, gently fold in Cool Whip™. Place mixture in a freezer safe container and freeze for at least 24 hours prior to serving.

- Remove from freezer and uncover at least 45 minutes (30 minutes small batch) prior to serving if you want to enjoy using a straw. If using spoons, ice cream can be enjoyed immediately.

> **Garnish Ideas:** Whipped Cream, Brown Sugar, Ground Cinnamon & Vanilla Sugar Wafer Cookies

FROSTY CAPPUCCINO

Ingredients

Large Batch	Small Batch
1 Gallon Chocolate Ice Cream	2 Cups Chocolate Ice Cream
16 oz. Cool Whip™	½ Cup Cool Whip™
1 ½ Tbs. Coffee Extract	½ Tsp. Coffee Extract
2 Tsp. Ground Cinnamon	½ Tsp. Ground Cinnamon

Instructions

- Remove ice cream and Cool Whip™ from freezer ahead of time. Cool Whip™ should be completely thawed before using. Ice cream should be soft enough to mix with an electric hand mixer. In an extra large mixing bowl, blend ice cream until smooth. Combine coffee extract and ground cinnamon with ice cream and mix until fully blended. Using a spatula, gently fold in Cool Whip™. Place mixture in a freezer safe container and freeze for at least 24 hours prior to serving.

- Remove from freezer and uncover at least 45 minutes (30 minutes small batch) prior to serving if you want to enjoy using a straw. If using spoons, ice cream can be enjoyed immediately.

> **Garnish Ideas:** Whipped Cream, Cocoa Powder, Chocolate Syrup & Chocolate Wafer Cookies

HAPPY BIRTHDAY TO ME!

Ingredients

Large Batch	Small Batch
1 Gallon Vanilla Ice Cream	2 Cups Vanilla Ice Cream
16 oz. Cool Whip™	½ Cup Cool Whip™
1 ½ Tbs. Cake Batter Extract	½ Tsp. Cake Batter Extract

Instructions

- Remove ice cream and Cool Whip™ from freezer ahead of time. Cool Whip™ should be completely thawed before using. Ice cream should be soft enough to mix with an electric hand mixer. In an extra large mixing bowl, blend ice cream until smooth. Combine cake batter extract with ice cream and mix until fully blended. Using a spatula, gently fold in Cool Whip™. Place mixture in a freezer safe container and freeze for at least 24 hours prior to serving.

- Remove from freezer and uncover at least 45 minutes (30 minutes small batch) prior to serving if you want to enjoy using a straw. If using spoons, ice cream can be enjoyed immediately.

> **Garnish Ideas:** Whipped Cream & Sprinkles

Ingram Content Group UK Ltd.
Milton Keynes UK
UKRC041015070623
423030UK00001B/1